Amelia Evans is playwright and dramaturg. Her writing credits include: *The Myth Project: Twin* (Arthur/MTC NEON); *Lyrebird* (Tamarama Rock Surfers); *Waltzing Woolloomooloo: The Tale of Frankie Jones* (Arthur); and *The Saturated World* (Melbourne Fringe). As dramaturg, her credits include: *The Sea Project* (Arthur/Griffin Theatre Company); *Wrecking* (TRS); *Dirtyland* (Arthur/The Spare Room); and *Private View* (NIDA, Theatreworks). Upcoming projects include a play for 5–13-year-olds, *Mad as a Cute Snake,* the sequel to *Cut Snake*. She graduated from NIDA in 2010.

Dan Giovannoni is an award-winning playwright and theatre-maker from Melbourne. His writing credits include: *Wrecking*, *Two by Two*, *imagine title here: the book of being young*, and the jukebox musical *Digging Down*. He is also a teaching artist, and has worked with companies such as Back to Back, Theatre of Speed, No Show and AWESOME Arts. Dan's education notes for *Cut Snake* were awarded Best Education Resource by Drama Victoria.

Cut Snake was awarded the Best Emerging Writer award at the 2011 Melbourne Fringe Festival and Best Performance by a Theatre Company for VCE Drama by Drama Victoria. It was shortlisted for the Rodney Seaborn Playwrights award, and nominated for two Green Room awards (Best Independent Ensemble and New Work for the Australian Stage).

Catherine Davies as Kiki, Kevin Kiernan-Molloy as Jumper and Julia Billington as Bob in the 2013 ARTHUR production of *Cut Snake* at Rock Surfers Theatre Company, Sydney. (Photo: John Feely)

CUT SNAKE

Dan Giovannoni and Amelia Evans
with Paige Rattray

in collaboration with Tom Hogan,
Catherine Davies, Kevin Kiernan-Molloy,
Julia Billington and Marcus McKenzie

Currency Press, Sydney

CURRENCY TEENAGE SERIES

First published in 2014
by Currency Press Pty Ltd,
PO Box 2287, Strawberry Hills, NSW, 2012, Australia.
enquiries@currency.com.au
www.currency.com.au

Copyright: *Cut Snake* © Dan Giovannoni and Amelia Evans 2014;
Teachers' Notes © Dan Giovannoni, 2013; Photographs © John Feely

COPYING FOR EDUCATIONAL PURPOSES
The Australian Copyright Act 1968 (Act) allows a maximum of one chapter or 10% of this book, whichever is the greater, to be copied by any educational institution for its educational purposes provided that that educational institution (or the body that administers it) has given a remuneration notice to Copyright Agency Limited (CAL) under the Act. For details of the CAL licence for educational institutions contact CAL, Level 15, 233 Castlereagh Street, Sydney, NSW, 2000; tel: within Australia 1800 066 844 toll free; outside Australia 61 2 9394 7600; fax: 61 2 9394 7601; email: info@copyright.com.au

COPYING FOR OTHER PURPOSES
Except as permitted under the Act, for example a fair dealing for the purposes of study, research, criticism or review, no part of this book may be reproduced, stored in a retrieval system, or transmitted in any form or by any means without prior written permission. All enquiries should be made to the publisher at the address above.
Any performance or public reading of *Cut Snake* is forbidden unless a licence has been received from the authors or the authors' agent. The purchase of this book in no way gives the purchaser the right to perform the play in public, whether by means of a staged production or a reading. All applications for public performance should be addressed to the authors c/- Currency Press.

Cataloguing-in-publication data for this title is available from the National Library of Australia website: www.nla.gov.au

Typeset for Currency Press by Dean Nottle.
Cover illustration and design by Emma Vine.

Currency Press acknowledges the Traditional Owners of the Country on which we live and work. We pay our respects to all Aboriginal and Torres Strait Islander Elders, past and present.

Contents

Cut Snake — 1

Teachers' Notes — 26

Above: Catherine Davies as Kiki Coriander and Julia Billington as Trix The Snake. Below: Kevin Kiernan-Molloy as Jumper and Julia Billington as Bob in the 2013 ARTHUR production of *Cut Snake* at Rock Surfers Theatre Company, Sydney. (Photos: John Feely)

First Production

Cut Snake was first produced by ARTHUR on 20 September 2011 at the Sydney Fringe Festival, in a secret location somewhere near the Seymour Centre, Sydney, with the following cast:

Bob	Julia Billington
Kiki	Catherine Davies
Jumper	Kevin Kiernan-Molloy

Director / Devisor, Paige Rattray
Writers, Amelia Evans and Dan Giovannoni
Producer, Belinda Kelly
Sound Designer / Devisor, Tom Hogan

Time travel invented by Scott Sandwich

Characters

    Kiki Coriander
    Bob
    Jumper
    Narrator
    Mrs Broccolini, a teacher
    Trix
    Feelings
    Lady Godiva
    Band of Gypsies
    Tim
    Fairy
    Jesus
    John Lennon
    Soldier 1
    Eve
    Adam
    James Turner

The performer playing Kiki also plays the Teacher and Eve.

The performer playing Jumper also plays Lady Godiva, Tim, Adam, Jesus, John Lennon, Soldier 1 and James Turner.

The performer playing Bob also plays Trix, a Band of Gypsies and Feelings.

They all play the Narrator as specified.

In the original version Bob was performed by a female.

Style

The play was devised by performers, writers, director and composer—the text being only one component of the theatrical world. The stage directions included in the text describe the movement/dance devised for the original production and should be seen as a launching point for future productions to interpret and re-imagine.

THE START

We're in a dark and smoky cabaret lounge—a dimly lit underground wonderland. The NARRATOR takes to the stage, steps up to the microphone and draws a quiet breath. He eyeballs the audience...

Narrator (J) Ladies, gentlemen and all those in between. Please put one hand like this...

He holds up his left hand.

And another like th s.

And his right...

And smack them together over and over for our opening act—Kiki Coriander and Trix the snake!

KIKI and TRIX perform their one-woman, one-snake cabaret, a high-energy double-act. They swing and roll and twirl.

BOB walks through the audience.

Bob Excuse me. Excuse me.

He find finds his way to the side of the stage. He motions to KIKI and she stops dancing.

He whispers the terrible news to her. She falls. JUMPER catches her, then puts her to her feet. She looks at BOB.

We jump back in time to the moment of the bus crash.

THE BUS CRASH

JUMPER is on a rickety old bus, heading into the mountains. He's feeling a little queasy.

Behind him, the other PERFORMERS are also on the bus—rickety and wild.

Jumper Don't ever let people tell you that getting out of bed and taking life by the balls helps cure a hangover... If you get out of bed, your hangover takes you by the balls and before you know it, the most important bus trip of your entire European adventure is compromised.

This might look like a fail—'cause I'm hung-over, again, with nothing to show for it except drunken photos in hostel bars. But this is actually a win. Because I'm going somewhere. I don't know where, but it's important. A Historical Site Of Some Sort. I bought a ticket. From a guy with a red hat. The bus came, we all got on. And even though right now all I want to do is get off and have a little nap in that bush over there… I need to suck it up. Pull it together. Because there will be something worth writing in this journal—I will remember something from this trip other than the taste of vomit in my mouth. I'm going to own it. I'm going to ride the waves of this hangover and own it. Yes, world. I am on a bus. Right now, I am on. A. Bus.

All three perform a movement piece inspired by the events of the bus crash.

The bus heads into the mountains. Tiny roads and sheer cliffs. We get to the top of this little rise, and before I can see what's on the other side, this mangy dog runs in front us. We swerve—'cause we don't want to hit him. Except we do hit him, and then we hit a tree. And then we go through the tree and through the metal road barrier, and the bus does this wicked little tumble over the edge of the cliff and smacks its head on a rock.

Then we roll. We're rolling. The woman in front of me dives on top of her kids but she misses them, and they get lost amongst smoke and bags and other bodies. I go to shove my journal under my hoodie, but because I let go of the seat I'm thrown headfirst into the wall, and my neck snaps. The windows smash, there's glass everywhere, and screaming. We're being tossed around like little chunks of meat, flesh ripping open. We roll, we're rolling, and when we finally hit the bottom…

JUMPER braces for impact—KIKI and BOB smash into him. They all turn out and see…

… the whole bus bursts into flames.

THE TELLING 1

KIKI and BOB sit on the roof of the cabaret lounge, the night sky before them. They dangle their feet over the edge, and watch the space between them and the sky.

Kiki When did it happen?
Bob 8:23 p.m. our time, 10:23 a.m. in Croatia. A Tuesday…
Kiki Is that his journal?
Bob His mum gave it to me; she thought we could read it together.

KIKI raises a toast.

Kiki To Jumper—wherever you are.
Bob To Jumper.

A shooting star rockets across the night sky.

Kiki Did you see that? A shooting star! You think it's a sign?
Bob Scientifically impossible.
Kiki But—
Bob Shooting stars don't exist, Kiki. That flash of light is merely the visible path of a meteoroid as it enters our atmosphere and becomes a meteor.
Kiki Well, maybe that meteor was a sign.

She picks up the journal sitting between them, and pauses before she opens it. She flicks through the pages, but instead of the words of wisdom she hoped for…

It's empty.

JUMPER'S STORY

JUMPER and KIKI perform a dumb show behind the NARRATOR as he tells the story.

Narrator (B) Jumper's story.
    Jumper was conceived during a wild electrical storm. His mum, Pam, was on a four-day bender at a bush doof with a travelling fire twirler named Guy. Guy shoved a jumper up his t-shirt and suggested they have a baby. Nine months later, Guy had twirled on, and little Jumper was born…
Kiki That's pretty weird.
Jumper No it's not.
Narrator (B) When Jumper was six, he met Kiki Coriander. Kiki lived with her grandpa above a costume shop and was always dressed as a super hero.
Jumper That's hell weird.
Kiki It is not!

Narrator (B) They started spending a lot of time together—they got along famously.
Jumper You always dance everywhere.
Kiki Your mum smells like wood and kisses people on the mouth.
Jumper Well, your grandpa's a Scientoiletist.
Kiki You've got a pet parrot that eats its own poo!
Jumper You want to get an ice-cream?
Kiki Yes!
Narrator (B) Jumper and Kiki went to school with Bob. Jumper and Bob made friends on the first day of Grade Five—a Monday—and best friends on day two—a Tuesday. It was Mrs Broccolini that brought them together.

MRS BROCCOLINI, a stern schoolmistress, raps a ruler on her palm.

Mrs Broccolini Jumper? Get up here. I want you to show everyone in the class what an excellent speller you are. I want you to show the class how you spell 'enough'.
Narrator (B) Jumper gets up—king of the class—picks up some chalk and writes:
Jumper E-N-U-F.

MRS BROCCOLINI cackles maniacally.

Mrs Broccolini Wrong. Again.
Jumper E-N-U-F-F.
Mrs Broccolini Again.
Narrator (B) She makes him do it / again and again.
Mrs Broccolini Again and again.
Narrator (B) And he gets it wrong / again and again.
Mrs Broccolini Again and again.

She cackles once more, JUMPER is retreating into his shell.

Narrator (B) So Bob—Mrs Broccolini's soon-to-be ex-favourite student—calls out:
Bob Oi! It's E-N-O-U-G-H!

JUMPER grins wildly and scribbles the word on the board.

MRS BROCCOLINI falls to the floor, screaming and wailing like a melting witch.

The boys high-five.

Narrator (K) After that Bob and Jump were thick as thieves—often times they went down the pier, and Bob fished while Jumper reckoned things:
Jumper Do you reckon if I ran fast enough, I could run on top of the water, like skipping stones?
Narrator (K) And Bob gave him answers:
Bob No.
Narrator (K) Which Jumper wasn't always sure of:
Jumper You sure?
Bob Scientifically and completely impossible.
Narrator (K) But he appreciated the help anyway:
Jumper Yeah, you're probably right—thanks, man.
Narrator (K) Jumper started spending less time with Kiki—not that she minded. I mean, why would she be jealous of a couple of boys and their stupid… questions? I don't care! She… doesn't care.

JUMPER and BOB perform The Question Game—a phat beatbox/ poetry slam where they ponder the largest questions known to man.

Bob If a trio is three, and a quartet is four, what is a group of 187?
Jumper Which is bigger: a super massive black hole? Or a fully massive black hole?
Bob How many years has man existed?
Jumper True or false—does heaven exist?
Bob Do you have an uncle named Terry?
Jumper Is a man just a boy who isn't sexy anymore?
Bob What is the sonic equivalent of every fruit at once?
Jumper Did I turn the oven off?
Bob Who would win a fight between a hippo and a horse?
Jumper How does the internet work?
Bob How do telephones work?
Jumper In the moment before you die do you just think, 'Oh well—I guess that's that'?
Bob Should I keep this baby?
Jumper If space goes on forever—does that mean there are aliens as big as planet Earth?
Bob Who would win in a fight between a horse and a hippo?
Jumper That's the million-dollar question.
Bob Could you ever fall back in love with Mel Gibson?

Jumper Could you beat your dad in a fight? What about Jesus? Could you beat him in a fight?
Bob What is the difference betwixt a hoof and a trotter?
Jumper True or false—does time travel exist?

> *BOB breaks the beat with a shining moment of boring practicality.*

Bob No.
Jumper Well, I think that it does.
Bob Impossible.
Jumper Why?
Bob Science.
Jumper Bob. Bob, Bob, Bob. Bob. Bob. Have you got your bombproof vest on?

> *BOB puts on his invisible bombproof vest.*

Bob Yep.
Jumper Good—because I'm about to drop a big one.

> *JUMPER drops a bomb—Boom!*

A sound has an echo. That's fact. An echo is just vibrations in air particles, impacting and resisting each other, getting smaller and smaller, until they come to rest. That's fact. Then the sound is lost forever. Right?

Wrong!

These particles have muscle memory, so it's a matter of activating them, reminding them of what they once were.

So those particles will never be still, and any sound we make is echoed, forever, until the world collapses back in on itself. Like a memory of something infinitely minute—the colour of your grandmother's scarf, the feel of carpet from your first house… they still hang around after however many years.

So if a sound is echoing forever, we need to recreate those vibrations in order to revisit those memories.

Part 1: The Base Notes—the weight of the past, the depth of the pond.

Part 2: The Middle Tones—the present, the surface of the pool.

Part 3: The Top Notes—the energy, the current of the future, taking the present and the past and making them something new, a river of time, my friend, that you can dive right on into.

We're so close— they're the right notes but we're missing something small…

Narrator (K) Jumper almost had Bob convinced, except at that moment… a snake appeared.

> *JUMPER sees TRIX from across the room. The lights dim, the mood shifts, and love is in the air. She transfixes him, and snakes her way toward him… (In the original production, TRIX was played by a hand, with two eyes drawn on the fingers and a green leg warmer worn on the arm.)*

Trix My name is Trix and I was bought in a market in India in 1943, when a 17-year-old Italian named Franco saw me. He was sso captivated by my eyes, thesse deep dark pools you ssimply cannot penetrate, that he had to have me. Sso he did. Until lasst week… when I ate him.

> *TRIX snaps at JUMPER.*

Jumper Whoa—you can talk?
Trix Of coursse I can talk.
Jumper Can I .. touch you?
Trix Whatever.

> *He reaches out a nervous hand and touches the snake's muscled body. He melts.*

Jumper You feel hell awesome. Your skin is so… scaly. And the muscles… It's like a party of muscles. I wanna go to that party. Haha.

> *He leans in, and she does too, and the two touch lips—or beaks—or whatever it is that snakes have. They pash wildly and obscenely for just a moment too long, then JUMPER pulls away.*

I've never met anyone like you… I—I know it seems way too early to call it—but I reckon I love you. You're just so… hot. The curve in your back. The way it softens through your mid-section, the way you flick your tail.

> *KIKI stumbles upon this scene and is a little… curious.*

Kiki Is that a talking snake?
Jumper Uh. Yep.
Kiki You look like you're in love with it.
Jumper Maybe I am.

Kiki That's pretty weird.
Jumper I know.
Kiki Yeah... Well, I'm pretty weird too.
Jumper Yeah. How?
Kiki Oh, I don't know—because I'm going to run away with the circus... star in a one-woman cabaret act, and fall in love with a bearded lady.
Jumper Well, Trix is named after Beatrix d'Este, who was like, the most beautiful and generally awesome princess of the whole Italiano Renaissance.
Kiki Well, I'm going to win Olympic gold in fencing.
Jumper Well, Trix can hypnotise shit. All kinds of shit.
Kiki I'm going to climb Mount Kilimanjaro with a band of gypsies and my bearded lady, we're gonna dance the tango at the peak and then move to a private island and keep dolphins as pets.

JUMPER is so seriously impressed by how weird this chick is that he forgets about TRIX altogether.

Jumper Whoa. That's pretty awesome...
Narrator (B) Jumper started to find Kiki and her plans strangely attractive. He started to have feelings. He started to wrestle with these feelings.

JUMPER wrestles with his FEELINGS for KIKI.

Feelings You like her!
Jumper No I don't.
Feelings You want to marry she, get a most comfortable job, move to a suburb and have millions of she babies!
Jumper I do not! I love Trix the snake!

FEELINGS triumphs over JUMPER, who falls to the ground weeping.

Narrator (B) Kiki also started to have feelings. She also started to wrestle with those feelings.
Feelings You like him!
Kiki No I don't.
Feelings You want to marry him, get a most comfortable job, move to a suburb and have millions of him babies!
Kiki I do not! I'm going to have an extraordinary life with the bearded lady!

FEELINGS triumphs over KIKI, who spits out a tooth she lost in the fight and starts bawling.

Narrator (B) Meanwhile Jumper's relationship with Trix was becoming more and more heated.

JUMPER comes home from a late night out, a little charged, and TRIX is nowhere to be found.

Jumper Trix! TRIIIIIIXY? Where are ya, babe? Oh—there ya'ar. You been out at the bars again, have ya? Don't you talk back to me—I'm a Man!

He hits out at TRIX, Stanley Kowalski style—but don't worry—it's not a real snake—it's just a sock... He feels bad anyway.

I'm sorry, babe. I only do it 'cause I love you—right? You just make me so crazy. So crazy.

Narrator (B) Jumper was conflicted.
Jumper I'm hell conflicted, hey.
Narrator (B) The situation was unbearable.
Jumper This is unbearable!
Narrator (B) Jumper had to do something.
Jumper I have to do something!
Narrator (B) What are you going to do?!
Jumper I'm gunna... I'm gunna... Go overseas. By myself. For ages!

KIKI is outraged.

Kiki Where?!
Jumper Europe. Asia!
Kiki Good. Fine. I'm glad.
Jumper Good. Fine. I'm glad too.

They turn away from each other.

One. Two. JUMPER looks back at her.

Kiki?
Kiki Yeah?
Jumper It'll probably be hell dangerous where I'm headed. Who knows if I'll even make it back...
Kiki Jumper, you're going on a Contiki tour.
Jumper Yeah, well... they won't let me take Trix on the bus with me, so... will you look after her till I get back? You could put her in your cabaret act—you'd like that, wouldn't you, Trix?
Trix Whatever.

Jumper   Please? I'd be hell grateful.

KIKI thinks about it a second, then sighs dramatically.

Kiki   Okay.

JUMPER and KIKI come close to one another—they look about to pash.

Jumper   And if anything should happen to me... promise you'll take her to the forests of India and set her free?

KIKI turns away outraged.

Thanks, Kik.

He goes to leave.

See ya, babes. Oh. I'm gunna keep a journal of all the amazing shit I do. It'll probably blow your minds. See ya in a few months. If you're lucky...

Narrator (B)   Jumper went to Bob's house to tell him the sweet news—

Jumper   Bob. Bobby, Bobcat?! I'm going to Europe, Asia!

Narrator (B)   But Bob wasn't at home—or at the pier—for Bob was at the zoo. He'd been secretly conducting an experiment to scientifically prove—once and for all:

Bob   The answer! To the million-dollar question!

Narrator (K)   Bob ran to Jumper's place to tell him the sweet news—

Bob   Jumper! Jumper cables? I've cracked it!

Narrator (K)   But Jumper was already on the plane to Europe, Asia. Where he got drunk in Paris, Madrid, Amsterdam... when a little dog ran in front of a bus...

KIKI'S STORY

KIKI teases TRIX with a rat. TRIX follows her like a dog.

Narrator (J)   After Jumper died, Kiki Coriander was going to set Trix free in the forests of India. But then their cabaret act was offered a two-year world tour!

KIKI's ears prick up.

Kiki   A two-year world tour? That'd be extraordinary, wouldn't it, Trix?

Trix   Whatever.

Kiki But I promised Jumper I'd set you free in the forests of India.

KIKI throws the rat into the air. TRIX catches and ingests it whole.

Trix I said whatever, bitch, I'm digesting a whole rat here. I can't be listening to your blah, blah, blah.

Narrator (J) Kiki was conflicted.

KIKI is extraordinarily conflicted.

Hell conflicted.

Kiki Hell conflicted? If anything I'm extraordinarily conflicted!

Narrator (J) Sorry—Kiki was extraordinarily conflicted. But deep down she knew exactly what she had to do. She told Trix to pack her bags—she was taking her *I* to the forests of.

Kiki On a two-year world tour!

Narrator (J) Ahhh—but you made a promise to Jumper?

Kiki So? Jumper's not here.

TRIX and KIKI look at him with crossed arms and raised eyebrows, united in sisterhood.

Narrator (J) ... So Kiki and Trix set out bringing their one-woman, one-snake act to the world.

They begin their cabaret act once again.

Narrator (B) Bulgaria, Pakistan, Laos—Kiki and Trix were a hit wherever they went.

One night, Kiki was out line dancing, when in walked...

LADY GODIVA, our bearded lady, springs to life, tossing a healthy beard over one shoulder. BOB as NARRATOR plays a southern ditty on the guitar.

Godiva My name is Chloe, but people call me Lady Godiva. I'm 36 years old, and was born in Austin, Texas. How long have I had the beard? Well, Mama said I came out full-bearded, hahaha! What was that? Am I in the circus? No, honey, I'm the CEO of a major multinational conglomerate enterprise—mmmk?... Anyways, one night after a hard old day at the office I walked into a bar and I saw...

GODIVA and KIKI start line dancing. On a turn they spot one another from across the room. The connection is instant, remarkable—this is L.O.V.E. They perform a warped but romantic line dance together, finishing with GODIVA running and jumping onto KIKI, her beard flowing down around KIKI's happy face.

Kiki Lady Godiva?
Godiva Yes, Kiki my dove?
Kiki Will you climb Mount Kilimanjaro with me, and dance the tango at the peak?
Godiva Well, of course I will, Kiki my dove!
Kiki We'll be extraordinary together, you and me, and live forever in the stars!
Godiva Uh-huh… Say, Kiki my dove?
Kiki Yes, Lady Godiva?
Godiva What do you reckon it'd be like to have a penis?

The music cuts. That wasn't part of KIKI's plan…

Narrator (B) Everything was going just as Kiki had planned. So Trix, Lady Godiva and Kiki jumped on a plane—and flew from Austin, Texas, to Mount Kilimanjaro, Tanzania. At the base they met:

A band of wild GYPSIES spring forth from the mountain. (In the original production, these were played by a gang of Barbies attached to a badminton racquet.)

Gypsies A hey-hey! We are a band of gypsies. To most everything and anything, we say, 'Why not?'
Kiki Hey, gypsies?
Gypsies A hey-hey!
Kiki Want to climb Mount Kilimanjaro with us?
Gypsies Why not?

They all begin the long trek up the mountain.

Narrator (B) Everything was going extraordinarily well! Except Trix started to lick people:

They stop.

Trix Just to see what they taste like. Mmm… tastes nice…

They keep trekking.

Narrator (B) And for some reason Lady Godiva kept stuffing bananas down her trousers:
Godiva Just to see what it feels like… Yeah, that feels nice.

They continue up to the very peak.

Narrator (B) On they went, one more rock, one more rock, until the rocks gave way to sky and finally they reached…
Kiki The peak! We made it!

She collapses.

We're like starfish clinging onto the side of the world. I feel like I could fall into the sky! Hey, gypsies?

Gypsies A hey-hey?
Kiki Play us a tango.
Gypsies Why not?

The GYPSIES play as KIKI grips onto GODIVA and leads her in a fast and passionate tango.

Godiva Kiki my dove—I got something I want to tell you.

KIKI dips GODIVA.

Kiki Tell me!
Godiva I'm going to get a sex change!

KIKI drops GODIVA.

Kiki What? Why?
Godiva I just think it'd be downright hot diggity to have myself a big old brand spankin' new penis... I've already got the beard for it, hahaha!
Kiki But then you wouldn't be a bearded lady.
Godiva No—I'll just be a regular old fella.
Narrator (B) This isn't exactly what Kiki had planned... but she's not going to let a little thing like a sex change get in her way.
Kiki Gypsies? Keep playing!
 ... Gypsies? Where are you?
Narrator (B) They look at Trix and notice she has a shape poking out of her belly. It's the exact shape of a band of gypsies.

We see the band of GYPSIES are indeed poking out of TRIX's sock stomach.

Trix I ate them. I was hungry. Whatever.

KIKI laughs hysterically, then falls. GODIVA catches her.

Godiva You feeling alright, Kiki my dove?
Kiki I'm on a rollercoaster and my stomach has dropped away. I have that rollercoaster feeling but I'm just standing here—not moving anywhere at all.
Godiva Okay...You want to dance some more tango?
Kiki I guess so.
Godiva This time, I think I better lead—seeing as I'm about to become a man.

> *They dance once more, except this time GODIVA leads. KIKI is like a sad doll, dragged from move to move. When it ends, GODIVA is gently stroking KIKI's inert head.*

Kiki I'm cold. I want my jumper.

BOB'S STORY

The NARRATOR is accompanied by the actor playing JUMPER on a gentle guitar or tinkling flute—setting the scene for the telling of:

Narrator (K) Bob's story! Bob was born on a Tuesday—just. It was 12:02—the witching hour. Rain lashed at the windows.
Bob The rain didn't 'lash'.

> *The music cuts. The NARRATOR motions for it to begin again.*

Narrator (K) Bob was born on a Tuesday. It was raining. When he came out he was screaming.
Bob Unverified.

> *Cut. The NARRATOR glares at BOB, and the music begins again.*

Narrator (K) Bob was born in winter. He may or may not have been screaming. When he was three he believed he could fly so jumped off the pier and—
Bob I didn't 'believe' I could fly—you're embellishing. If you're going to embellish the story I may as well just tell this lot myself.
Narrator (K) Fine.
Bob I was born on November 5th, 1986. A Tuesday. When I was three I jumped off the pier into the river and broke my... my...
Narrator (K) ... leg.
Bob Yes, my leg. From years 5–17 I went to school. There's not much to say about that, other than I fell in love, twice. And twice I didn't find the courage to tell them.
Narrator (K) Ginny O'Halloran and Grace Marlowe.
Bob When I was 19, my friend Jumper died in a bus crash.
Narrator (K) His best friend—
Bob I wanted to be a pilot so I applied to the air force. I was rejected so became a policeman instead. That's where I met Ally. We got married and had two kids, Rex and / Grace.
Narrator (K) Grace.
Bob I know. Ally got pregnant with a third but she had a miscarriage. Rex became a... a... don't tell me... a...

The NARRATOR coughs.

Narrator (K)   … bricklayer.
Bob   I said don't tell me! Grace got knocked up at 16 so dropped out of school to have the baby, Tim. So I became a grandfather, see? Ally and me retired and went on a trip.
Narrator (K)   To Venice.
Bob   We saw six rats…
Narrator (K)   Was it beautiful?
Bob   It was okay.

Tim started school, now that's my grandson, see? Grace got divorced. Ally got cancer and died. I learnt how to cook. Every second weekend I took Tim, my grandson, fishing off the pier.

Then I forgot. I forgot a few other things but I can't remember what they were. Then I had a heart attack. I moved into a hospice and fell in love again, with Yvonne Sinclair. I got up the courage to tell her but she wasn't interested. Oh, I remember that.

Then I had another heart attack and died. It was a Tuesday. And that was that.

BOB walks away.

Narrator (K)   No, it wasn't.
Bob   Yes, it was.
Narrator (K)   No. You forgot the thing.
Bob   What thing?
Narrator (K)   You forgot the [*sotto voce*] fairy.
Bob   The what now? Speak up!
Narrator (K)   [*whispering in his ear*] The fairy, you were on the pier with Tim? You saw the fairy? Then you invented time travel and you saw Jesus and John—
Bob   Oh! I remember. Tuesday January 23rd, 2046. Weird shit always happens on Tuesdays. I was on the pier.
Narrator (K)   The same pier that…

She remembers she's not supposed to embellish.

Sorry.
Bob   Oh, go on
Narrator (K)   Bob was on the pier—now that's the very same pier he threw himself off as a three-year-old, the same pier he fished off with Jumper all those years ago.

Bob I was with Tim, now that's my grandson, see...

BOB and TIM are on the pier. They cast their lines, a gentle quiet between them.

Tim Grandpa? Do you reckon there could be a trout in there—as big as a sheep?

Bob No.

BOB gets a nip.

Tim You got something, Grandpa?

Bob Give us a hand, Timmy, my arms aren't what they used to be.

Tim Looks like it's a big one! I reckon it's a trout as big as a sheep!

Bob Scientifically and completely impossible!

TIM sees something.

Narrator (K) But Tim didn't hear his grandpa. Because he'd seen something.

Tim Grandpa.

Bob I'm losing him, Tim!

Tim Grandpa.

Narrator (K) Bob looks up. He sees something that makes him forget his rod altogether. It goes flying out of his arms and plunges deep into the water. But he doesn't care—because the thing he's seen is—

A FAIRY. A real life, actual fairy, that flies out over the river, then back again, and lingers in front of their faces long enough for them to know beyond doubt... that it's real. (In the original, the performers saw the fairy, then become the fairy.)

They return to themselves on the boat.

Tim It's really there, isn't it, Grandpa?

Bob It really is...

Narrator (K) Bob went back to the hospice. He'd seen something:

Bob Scientifically and completely impossible.

The music again.

Narrator (K) He started to wonder about other things he'd always thought scientifically and completely impossible. He started to wonder about something Jumper had reckoned all those years ago...

Bob If a fairy is real, if fairies are fact—would you shut that thing up?

The music stops—for good this time.

If a fairy is real, then science has its magic too.

The Big Bang—a beginning that matters, with anti-matter, shooting vibrations in every direction, space and stars expanding and pushing... and it's still going. We are living the echo, after millions and billions and trillions of years. So those particles will never be still, and any sound we make is echoed, forever, until the world collapses back in on itself with the Big Suck.

But this is science, and even science needs its magic. Harmony. It's harmony, the right notes in the right order at the right time. Maybe Jumper was right.

Stage one: the surface, the base notes...

He uses one PERFORMER to sing a bass note.

Good. Now we need the middle tones, the... the depth of the pool.

BOB sings the middle note.

We need the top notes, the current, the magic.

And a third PERFORMER sings the top notes.

We need it louder, we need it better, we need it more theatrical, so I can dive into the current of time.

The sound builds. The PERFORMERS are flung through the current of time and BOB—crusty old-man-BOB—dives forward, headfirst, through time... into the past!

THE TIME TRAVEL

BOB arrives in 10 BC, and finds himself face to face with...

Bob Are you Jesus?
Jesus Yeah, man.
Bob I'm Bob. I'm from the future. I invented time travel.
Jesus Right on. I'm eating dates.
Bob I've never had a date before.
Jesus You want to share a date with me, man?
Bob Okay.

JESUS shares his dates with BOB.

Jesus How did you know my name?
Bob You're pretty famous.

Jesus Right on.
Bob Can I get a photo?

> *He snaps a selfie with him.*

Jesus Peace be with you, brother.

> *They sing again, and BOB dives back into time and arrives in 1968, face to face with…*

Bob Are you John Lennon?
John Yeah, man, who are you?
Bob I'm Bob, I'm from the future.
John That's cool.
Bob Are you eating a sticky date pudding?
John Yeah. With double cream.
Bob Can I have a bit?

> *He shakes his head 'no', his mouth too full to answer.*

Bob Can I get a photo?
John Oh. Go on, but just don't tell Yoko.

> *He snaps a selfie with him. YOKO is not impressed.*

Peace be with you, man.

> *BOB dives back into time and arrives on a battlefield in 1943. One SOLDIER screams in agony and holds his leg. ANOTHER throws a grenade before getting shot a lot. It's intense.*

Soldier 1 Aaaaaaagh! Aaaaaaaaaahgghhhh! AAAAAAAGGGHHHH!
Bob Can I get a photo?

> *The SOLDIERS smile and give the peace sign as he snaps an arm-reach photo with them.*

Soldier 1 Hey!

> *BOB dives back into time and arrives at the beginning of time, face to face with ADAM and EVE. When he enters they grab whatever they can to cover their privates.*

Bob Are you guys…?
Eve Who else would we be? Look around—it's the beginning of time.
Bob Did all that stuff really happen? With the snake and the apple?
Eve Does everyone know about that?
Bob Oh, yes.
Eve What are people saying?

Bob That you destroyed the utopian unity between the sexes, made woman subordinate to man and forced her to endure painful childbirth.
Eve Are you serious?! That snake—that snake hypnotised me, then tricked me! Tell them, Adam… Adam?
Adam I'm staying out of this.
Eve Oh, yeah, that'd be right, Mr 'Is it nice? Can I have a bite?'
Adam Aw, c'mon, babe—
Eve I just wish you'd have the guts to stand up to him for once!

BOB snaps a selfie with them and leaves.

He dives back into time and arrives in 2005. He's on a bus.

Bob Is this seat taken?

BOB sits down next to a seedy-looking 18-year-old—JUMPER. They bobble along, BOB staring at his friend.

Jumper Ugh.

He could have had any other seat, all to himself—but of course, he picks the one next to mine. He keeps… sideways looking at me.

He catches BOB looking. BOB smiles weirdly.

Great—a full-on certified weirdo. We hit a bump in the road, my stomach flips and I can taste bile. I'm about to get up, admit defeat, have a cheeky vomit and a nap in that bush over there, when he pulls out his camera.

BOB pulls out his camera.

Jumper I'm trapped now—I force a smile as he starts flicking through the photos of him and some kid—
Bob Tim. That's my grandson, see?
Jumper Then one of him with some dude dressed like Jesus, then Jesus with sunglasses. He keeps pointing at the pictures saying:
Bob World War Two…
Jumper I'm smiling and nodding but it's hell weird.
Bob Adam and Eve.
Jumper Cool, man.

Then he points at my camera and says:
Bob Let's see yours?
Jumper Oh. Nothing to see, mate—just me drunk in a bunch of places.

Bob Show me.
Jumper So I get out my camera and I'm clicking through—there's me drunk in Paris, hung-over in Madrid.
Bob Where was that?
Jumper Oh. Amsterdam. I think.
Bob And this?
Jumper Just a pub. O'Halloran's. It's for my mate. A personal joke kind of thing.
Bob Who are these girls?
Jumper Straight up, dude. I don't remember. I was gone… They're in a few photos actually. Here in Manchester.
Bob She liked you.
Jumper I don't know about that.
Bob Bit of a looker too. Who's that?
Jumper Javier—I think that's how you say his name—I hitched a ride across Spain in his truck.
Bob Looks like he'd have a story or two.
Jumper Ha. Yeah. He did… Oh, this guy—in London, running for the Tube and then the doors close right on his face and all he says is, 'Delightful'.

They laugh.

Bob You written any of this down?
Jumper Nah.
Bob You should.
Jumper You reckon?
Bob Yeah. I reckon.
Jumper I keep clicking through, he keeps asking questions and you know—I reckon this is the raddest dude I've met this whole trip. It goes on like that for an hour, then he says:
Bob This is my stop.
Jumper Yeah. Cool, man.
  Then he looks at me. Right in my eyes…

  BOB stares at him.

  It's weird. He sees my journal, grabs it, and scribbles something at the back. Then shakes my hand and says:
Bob Goodbye.
Jumper Yeah. See ya, dude.
  And he gets off. I look back at him but then the bus turns a

corner, heading up into the mountains, and he's gone.

> The PERFORMERS, except JUMPER, repeat the movement of the first bus crash.

We keep bumping along—windy roads and sheer cliffs—but now, my headache's cleared and the air's fresh. I flick back through my photos and suddenly I remember who those chicks were. I've got my journal in my hands so I get a pen and write down their names, where we met. Then the memories start flooding back and I have this urge to get it all down, make it real. It's hard, the suspension on the bus is shot, and my handwriting's shaky, but I don't care—I write and write and write till I realise I haven't even looked at what the old dude wrote—so I flick to the back and I read:

> He reads what BOB wrote, then looks up. He braces for impact—
> KIKI jumps onto his shoulders, BOB jumps onto his stomach—
> they see the bus burst into flames.

THE TELLING—TAKE 2

KIKI and BOB sit on the roof of the cabaret lounge, the night sky before them. They dangle their feet over the edge, and watch the space between them and the sky.

Kiki When did it happen?
Bob 8:23 p.m. our time. 10:23 a.m. in Croatia. A Tuesday...
Kiki Is that his journal?
Bob His mum gave it to me; she thought we could read it together.

> KIKI reads from it, aloud.

Kiki 'Francesca and Sophia—from Florence. We were staying in the same hostel in Liverpool the night that guy in our dorm woke up screaming.'
Jumper JESUS SHIT!
Kiki And then projectile vomited all over himself.'
Bob Grossss.
Jumper It reeked.
Kiki 'Francesca asks me, "Do you, how you say, consume the alcohol?" Must've said, "Hell yes", because next thing I know I'm shirtless, hugging a dude called Terry with prison tatts—he's crying and I'm singing.'

Jumper 'Rooney! Whoareya? Whoareya?'
Kiki 'I remember being in a pub in Glasgow and suddenly realising everyone spoke exactly like Itchy Arse Dude—' Who's Itchy Arse Dude?
Bob I don't know.
Jumper Yeah you do—he started chasing us on his bike? We were at the school gate and he was screaming.
Bob I can't remember.
Jumper Yeah, you do.
   Come on, Bobcat.
   KIKI and BOB are about to give up and continue reading.
   Come on, Bob.
Bob The Scot.
Jumper Yes!
Bob Yes—he had his hand down his pants and he was screaming.
Bob & Jumper [*together*] HEY—DO YOU KNOW HOW TO CURE AN ITCHY ARSE?
Bob And then Jumper saw Mrs Broccolini, so he goes:
Jumper 'Nah, but she does!'
Bob And he took off after her instead.
   They laugh. A little too long.
Kiki 'I remember I passed out on the last train to Paris, missed my stop and ended up in some scary-arse suburb with no money and no way to get back.'
Jumper Missed you then, Bob—you would've known what to do.
Bob Hopeless.
Kiki 'I remember finding a park and trying to sleep on a bench—when I looked up into the trees they were all lit up with tiny green lights—hundreds and hundreds of fireflies.'
Jumper You'd've loved that, Kiki. I thought of you.
Kiki 'I remember—'
   She stops reading. The writing has stopped.
   That's it.
   JUMPER backs away and leaves. BOB turns to the back of the book and sees what is written there—what he himself will write in about 60 years time. Just then, a shooting star rockets across the night sky.

Did you see that? A shooting star. You think it's a sign?
Bob Actually, Kiki, shooting stars don't really… I mean…
I don't know. Maybe.

They clink shot glasses.

To Jumper.
Kiki To Jumper.

THEIR LIFE STORIES. AGAIN, BUT FASTER, AND A LITTLE BIT DIFFERENT

Narrator (B) Now, we all know the rules of time travel. You can't change the past without it affecting the future. So after Jumper died, Kiki Coriander and Trix the snake were offered a two-year world tour. But Kiki turns it down—she'd made a promise to Jumper. So she set Trix free in the forests of India.
Kiki See ya, Trix. Nice working with you.
Trix Whatever.

KIKI begins her one-woman (no-snake) act.

Narrator (B) She still goes travelling—to Bulgaria, Pakistan, Laos. One night, she's on stage when in walks a bearded lady.

A dumb show of their relationship.

They still have a whirlwind affair, but this time Kiki notices little things—like the fact that she is always and forever putting vegetables down her trousers.

Kiki decides before she asks Lady Godiva to climb Mount Kilimanjaro she'll win gold in Olympic fencing.

LADY GODIVA turns into JAMES TURNER, and he and KIKI face off—fencing-style.

Kiki En garde!
Narrator (B) She's invincible! No-one can touch her—no-one except:
James My name is James Turner—I'm just a regular bloke.

Their fancy fencing turns into a tasty tango. This is L.O.V.E. Again. But for real this time. They keep dancing the tango, all the way through the following:

Narrator (B) She doesn't win gold.
Kiki I came 34th.
Narrator (B) But for some reason, she doesn't mind. One day she

looks at her stomach and realises:

JAMES lifts her, spinning splits.

Kiki There's a baby in there!

Narrator (B) So she makes a suggestion she never thought she'd make:

Full starfish lift in the sky.

Kiki Let's move to a suburb!

JAMES drops KIKI and advances on the audience with a defensive parry.

James So I'm out in the backyard practising my flunges, when out of nowhere this big bloody snake appears, tries to go me! So I pull a passata sotto—bit of a defensive parry—I'm about to go full flunge when—

Kiki Stop!

A pregnant KIKI waddles between JAMES and the snake, because…

It's Trix!

Trix Sssso I'm back. Whatever. Don't make it a thing.

James After that, Kiki and Trix started performing together again.

Kiki We've still got plans to go to Tanzania, climb Mount Kilimanjaro, but we also do the dishes, read the Sunday paper and:

She births Cardigan on a turn—then he's five.

Walk our little boy, Cardigan, to school.

James He wears dresses and tiaras and reckons he's going to be the first man to dance the tango on Mars… He's a pretty cool little dude.

Narrator (B) In this life—which is sometimes ordinary and sometimes extraordinary—Kiki laughs a lot.

JAMES and KIKI share an ordinary family moment, and clear the stage, leaving BOB—crusty old man BOB—who hobbles up nice and close to the audience.

Bob I was born on November 5th, 1986. A Tuesday.

My friend—my best friend, Jumper, died when I was 19.

I met Ally in the police force and we had two kids, Rex and Grace. Every now and then we'd take them over to my friend Kiki's house and they'd play with her little boy, Cardigan. Ally called

Kiki's 'The Menagerie' but I know secretly she loved it… When she had a miscarriage it was Kiki she talked to.

When we retired we took a trip to—now don't tell me—you come in on the train and all of a sudden there's just water on both sides of you—it's like you're flying. Venice! We saw six rats. It was beautiful.

Then Ally got cancer… and she died.

Once, when I was fishing with Tim—that's my grandson, see?—we saw a fairy. Actually, a fairy. Then I invented time travel! I went back and I met Christ and John Lennon, Adam and Eve… and visited my old friend, Jumper, on the day he died. I wrote in his journal—the answer to the million-dollar question.

Then I had a heart attack. I moved into a hospice and fell in love again, with Yvonne Sinclair. I got up the courage to tell her but she wasn't interested. I had another heart attack and died.

It was a Tuesday.

And that was that.

He turns to shuffle off, but stops, and turns back.

Oh. I almost forgot. The real question is—the million-dollar question is:

Who would win in a fight between a hippo and a horse?

A HIPPO and a HORSE smack down in the ring. It's rough, it's loud, it's huge. After a tough fight… the HORSE is victorious— who would've thought it?

THE END

Cut Snake Teachers' Notes

TAKE ANOTHER LOOK AT LIFE AND SAY: HELL YES!

WE WANT THIS PLAY TO CHANGE THE WORLD.
AND IF NOT THE WORLD, THEN JUST EVERYONE IN IT.

Cut Snake is a magical, high-energy piece of contemporary, non-naturalistic Australian theatre, collaboratively created by independent theatre company ARTHUR. These notes are designed to help students and teachers of drama and theatre studies delve deeper into the world of *Cut Snake*. Working with these notes will help students and teachers understand what the team at ARTHUR were thinking as they put the show together.

If you have any other questions, you can contact the team at ARTHUR below.

Email: belinda@arthurproductions.com.au
Twitter: @arthurprod
Facebook: facebook.com/makersofplay
Website: www.arthurproductions.com.au

Notes prepared by Dan Giovannoni for ARTHUR.

Thanks to Megan Twycross for her feedback, support and additional notes.

BEFORE THE SHOW

THE WORLD OF *CUT SNAKE*

WHAT DO YOU THINK?

- In small groups brainstorm and discuss all the meanings of the phrase 'cut snake'. The following will help you with your discussion:
    - When do you use this expression? In what contexts?
    - What is the expression used to describe?
    - Is the expression used as a verb? A noun?
- Using the discussion, think about the title of the play and what you think the show might be like or about.

THE STORY

Cut Snake begins with Jumper narrating his own death in a bus accident in Europe-Asia. After his death, his journal—which he promised to write in every day to record his extraordinary experiences—is returned to his two best friends, Kiki and Bob, but it's empty. Jumper hasn't written a word. We skip back in time and see how Kiki, Bob and Jumper became friends, and why Jumper decided to travel to Europe-Asia in the first place. The play charts the effect his death has on Kiki and Bob.

We then pick up again after Jumper's death and see Kiki's story. Kiki blindly chases a life full of extraordinary experiences. She and Jumper's pet snake, Trix, perform their cabaret act all over the world. She climbs Mount Kilimanjaro with a band of gypsies and falls in love with a bearded lady named Lady Godiva. But all of her experiences are marred in some way—the snake eats the gypsies, the bearded lady wants to become a man… and suddenly the extraordinary life Kiki wanted to lead is leaving her cold.

Then we see Bob's life story. Bob spends his whole life focused on practical things. He gets married, has kids, does his job, and then dies—an ordinary life. Or so he'd like to believe. In reality he struggles to reconcile an extraordinary experience he once had: he and his grandson Tim see a fairy. Remembering his best mate, Jumper, who always chased adventure, Bob embarks on a mission to honour Jumper and invent time travel—to great success. He manages to visit Adam and Eve, John Lennon and Jesus… and then, finally, his best friend Jumper on the day that he died. In a final goodbye to his best friend, Bob convinces Jumper to write his memories and experiences down in his journal—and then leaves a secret note for him on the back page. After Bob leaves, Jumper dies all over again.

This time, when Jumper's journal is returned, Kiki and Bob find that although Jumper didn't have the capital-'i'-Important experiences he had planned, they were still worthwhile adventures. They are also reminded that he hadn't forgotten them. They still go on to live their lives—but this time a little differently. We watch as Kiki foregoes Mount Kilimanjaro and instead becomes an Olympic fencer. She meets James Turner, has a baby (Cardigan) and moves to the suburbs. Bob learns that you can have pretty extraordinary experiences if you let yourself, and so the rest of his life is lived in the knowledge that he should probably just say HELL YES a little more (which he does). Kiki recognises that not everything in her life has to be extraordinary—in fact, there might be something extraordinary waiting for her deep inside her ordinary suburban life.

In the final moment of the play, we learn what Bob's secret message to Jumper was in the back of the journal—he finally worked out the answer to a question that had puzzled them as kids: who would win in a fight between a hippo and a horse?

Kevin Kiernan-Molloy as Jumper and Catherine Davies as Kiki Coriander in the 2013 Arthur production of *Cut Snake* at Rock Surfers Theatre Company, Sydney. (Photo John Feely)

BEFORE YOU GO

Cut Snake has been performed in courtyards, pubs, cabaret bars, indoors, outdoors… anywhere a performance space can be made.

WHAT DO YOU THINK?

- How do you think the location of the performance influences an audience's understanding of a play? Give examples from your own experience.
- Are there places around your home or school that you think would be suitable to stage a piece of theatre?
    - What are some of the considerations you need to make if you were to stage a show in the place you have chosen?
    - What kind of environment does your setting create for the audience?
    - What kind of performance would suit this location?
    - What would be the benefits/problems of staging something in this location?
    - Would you stage a group devised or ensemble performance in this location?

ENSEMBLE THEATRE

The play script of *Cut Snake* was devised by the writers, director, performers and composer. This means that there are elements of the production, such as the movement sequences, that can only be replicated by this specific team. Stage directions are open to interpretation and experimentation by any other performers of this script. This can be said about any production after it has had its first performances.

WHAT DO YOU THINK?

- Read the note on 'Style' from the writers at the start of the play.
- After reading the note on 'Style' choose any stage direction and identify and describe what you expect to see in the production based on the stage directions.
- After seeing the production, compare and contrast the prediction that you made with the performance that you saw.
- Evaluate how different your expectations were from the final product.

MAGIC REALISM

A key aspect of the play is the world of *Cut Snake*. The play is set in a slightly altered version of the real world, where things are almost like normal, but not quite. This setting allows for the strange to become normal, for magical things to happen and for impossible things to be possible. In this way, the world of the play contains many elements of Magic Realism.

WHAT DO YOU THINK?

- What do you know about Magic Realism?
- How might this style sit alongside or be an example of non-naturalism?
- Do you know of any other plays/films/books that might fit into the category of Magic Realism?

REVIEWS AND PREVIOUS PRODUCTIONS

Cut Snake has had a number of productions since it premiered in 2011 at the Sydney Fringe Festival (2011)—the Melbourne Fringe Festival, in a tent next to Theatre Works in Melbourne, at Sydney's Bondi Pavilion, the Brisbane Festival, on tour throughout Regional NSW, and also in Kew, Hobart, Launceston and Canberra.

WHAT DO YOU THINK?

- Using the Internet, research the reviews and any other information you can about a previous production.
- After reading the material you have found in your research, identify and record what you have learnt about the production.
- List any questions you may now have about the production.
- Describe what you are expecting when you see the production.

THE TEAM

The creative team have their own titles and area/s of expertise and training, such as writer, director or producer. They are credited as devisors, too, because they all contributed to the making of it.

Director/Devisor
Paige Rattray
Writers/Devisors
Amelia Evans and Dan Giovannoni
Producer
Belinda Kelly
Composer/Devisor
Tom Hogan
Performers
Julia Billington, Catherine Davies and Kevin Kiernan-Molloy

A FEW MORE QUESTIONS BEFORE YOU SEE THE SHOW…

WHAT DO YOU THINK?

- After completing the previous activities, what are you now expecting from the performance?
- What are your plans for the end of Year Twelve?
    - Do you and your friends have plans for overseas travel?
    - Are you taking a gap year?
    - Are you going to uni?
    - Are you going to TAFE?
    - Are you going to schoolies? If so, where?
    - Why are you doing those things?
    - What's exciting about this next phase of your life?
- Are you expecting the play to 'teach' you anything? Do you think all plays have a lesson or a moral? Explain your answer.
- In *Cut Snake*, three actors play many roles. What are you expecting to see in relation to transformation?

BLINK AND YOU'LL MISS IT

Theatre is ephemeral. As soon as a line is said, it disappears—you can't rewind and listen to it again. It's also different every time it is performed. Sometimes a line is said in a way that makes it funny, other times in a way that makes it sad, other times someone's sneezing and you miss it altogether. This means that it's important to be curious—pay attention to details. It can be easy to just slip into the world of the play and forget you should be 'reading' the play as well as watching it.

At the end of the show, try and write a few things down—if you can't write them down, just have a conversation about them. Talking through it once will help you remember it tomorrow. Doing this after the show will help you write about what you saw at a later date.

An easy way to break it up is by thinking of:

- What you saw:
    - sets,
    - lights,
    - props,
    - costumes,
    - characters,
    - acting techniques,
    - the theatre space.
- What you heard:
    - music,
    - the script (dialogue, monologue, language),
    - songs,
    - body percussion.
- What you felt:
    - did the play move you?
    - was it funny?
    - did it make you angry, sad, or leave you bemused?
    - was it confusing, convoluted, or did it make sense?

It is important to have an opinion about what you have seen. Think about what was good and why it was good, and think about what may not have worked and why it did not work.

AFTER THE PERFORMANCE

ORDER OF SCENES AND THE NAMES OF SCENES

This is the order the scenes appear in:

1. THE START: KIKI'S CABARET
2. THE BUS CRASH
3. THE TELLING 1
4. JUMPER'S STORY
    a. JUMPER MEETS KIKI
    b. JUMPER MEETS BOB
    c. JUMPER & BOB'S BIG QUESTIONS
    d. JUMPER HALF INVENTS TIME TRAVEL
    e. JUMPER MEETS TRIX
    f. JUMPER & KIKI WRESTLE WITH THEIR FEELINGS
    g. JUMPER LEAVES FOR EUROPE-ASIA.
5. KIKI'S STORY
    a. KIKI & TRIX GO ON TOUR
    b. KIKI MEETS A BEARDED LADY
    c. KIKI CLIMBS A MOUNTAIN
    d. KIKI DANCES THE TANGO (HAPPY)
    e. KIKI'S PLANS ARE FOILED
    f. KIKI DANCES THE TANGO (SAD)
6. BOB'S STORY
    a. BOB TELLS HIS LIFE STORY
    b. BOB SEES A FAIRY
    c. BOB INVENTS TIME TRAVEL
        i. BOB MEETS JESUS
        ii. BOB MEETS JOHN LENNON
        iii. BOB VISITS WW1
        iv. BOB MEETS ADAM & EVE
        v. BOB MEETS JUMPER ON THE DAY HE DIED
7. THE TELLING 2
8. THEIR LIFE STORIES, AGAIN—BUT FASTER AND A LITTLE BIT DIFFERENT

WHAT DO YOU THINK?

- These scene titles help to tell the story. Reflecting on the performances what images, thoughts, ideas or feelings do the scene titles evoke for you?
- What do they tell you about the story and its structure? Is the structure linear? Non-linear? Realistic? Non-realistic? Justify your answer.
- Divide the class into small groups and allocate each group a scene, or series of scenes (if possible, allocate each group one character's story). Complete the following activities:
  - Using tableau (freeze-frame), represent each scene title (not what happens in the scene).
  - Present each scene in order using the Brechtian technique of placards/signs.
  - Extend the tableaus into short vignettes where the only dialogue comes from the title of the scene (for example, for 'Bob sees a fairy', the dialogue might be: 'I've seen a fairy!')
  - After creating the dialogue for each vignette use transitions to move between each scene.

WORKING WITH SCRIPT: 'THE BUS CRASH'

Reread Jumper's opening monologue from the start of the play and complete the following activities.

WHAT DO YOU THINK?

- How does this direct address from Jumper in the opening scenes help establish an actor-audience relationship?
- What theatrical styles and conventions are used in this approach? Analyse and describe the effect of each of these.
- What is the mood established by this monologue? How did the use of sound help communicate this mood?
- In what ways did you see a transformation of place occur in this scene? What expressive skills were used to help this?

WORKING WITH SCRIPT: 'BOB'S STORY' TAKEN FROM 'THEIR LIFE STORIES, AGAIN, BUT FASTER, AND A LITTLE BIT DIFFERENT'

Reread the second time Bob says this monologue and complete the following activities.

WHAT DO YOU THINK?

- How do you respond to this monologue? How does it make you feel? What does it make you think about? What images do you think of/imagine? What words in the monologue are the most evocative for you?
    - Choose five words or images based on the monologue.
    - Create a tableau for each of these words or images.
- Identify and evaluate how the performer's expressive skills help communicate pathos in this scene.
- Using your own life, write your own timeline, starting with birth, and going through to the end of your life.
    - Mark the important or significant moments.
    - Identify what makes these moments significant or important.
    - Imagine what will happen to you after you finish school and mark the significant events on the timeline.
    - Try and keep the facts simple, but embellish the important bits.
    - Share your timeline with a partner.
    - In pairs, choose one of the timelines to enact in a one-minute life cycle. This might be a series of vignettes, or freeze-frames.

WORKING WITH THE SCRIPT: 'KIKI CLIMBS A MOUNTAIN'

WHAT DO YOU THINK?

Look carefully at the image from 'Kiki climbs a mountain'. The image depicts (left to right) Lady Godiva, Kiki, Trix, the narrator, and the band of gypsies.

- Analyse the image and evaluate the actors' use of expressive skills.
- Identify a theme in *Cut Snake* and describe how it is present in this image.
- In this scene dialogue, narration and physical movement combine to tell the story.
  - Evaluate the actors' ability to sustain their characters whilst speaking and moving in time.
- How is the performance style of non-naturalism demonstrated in this image?
- Analyse and evaluate how elements of production (stagecraft elements) are used in this image to contribute to the mood of the scene?

WORKING WITH SCRIPT: 'THE TIME TRAVEL'

This scene shows Bob travelling through a number of time periods, and then finally arriving on Jumper's bus just before Jumper dies.

WHAT DO YOU THINK?

- Identify three theatrical conventions in this scene and discuss how they support a major theme in the play.
- At the end of this scene (when Bob arrives on the bus), a piece of music we've already heard starts playing (song title: 'The Bus Crash Revisited'). When did we hear it before? In what way does hearing this music again contribute to the pathos or mood of the scene?
- Give an example of where Magic Realism is evident in this scene. Evaluate the effectiveness of the use of Magic Realism in the scene.
- Evaluate how the actors use expressive skills to create the transformation of place? Identify any other theatrical conventions that support this transformation.
- In what way is transformation of object evident in this scene? Was it successful? What expressive skills supported this transformation?

WORKING WITH SCRIPT: 'KIKI'S CABARET'

Identify the dramatic elements, performance styles and theatrical conventions at play in the opening scene of *Cut Snake* ('Kiki's Cabaret').
You might want to do it in charts, such as these:

OPENING SCENE

Dramatic element	How is it used?	What is the effect?
Contrast	Contrasting a lively, energy-fuelled scene (the Cabaret performance) with a sad and mournful movement sequence (the falling/catching).	The pathos of the next scene—the bus crash—is increased because the audience have already gone on an emotional journey.

OPENING SCENE

Performance styles	How is it used?	What is the effect?
Non-naturalism	The opening address is from a narrator, who speaks in direct address to the audience.	The audience is instantly involved in the world of the play by being asked to applaud Kiki's cabaret act.

WORKING WITH SCRIPT: CHARACTER CHART

Use this example chart to detail the expressive skills used by each actor when playing their many characters.

Jumper, played by Kevin Kiernan-Molloy.
Costume: white singlet, suspenders, grey trousers (pant legs rolled up), bare feet.
Transformed into: Lady Godiva, Tim, Adam, Jesus, John Lennon, Soldier 1, James Turner.

CHARACTER	FACIAL EXPRESSION	VOICE	GESTURE	MOVEMENT
Jumper	Teenage scowl	Broad Australian accent, youthful, almost his natural voice.		
Chloe (Lady Godiva)		High-pitched, overly-effeminate contrasted with a deep, masculine tenor when transitioning to a male, caricatured accent (Texan).	Stroking her beard	Pointed toes
James Turner		Broad Australian accent, masculine sounding (deep)—similar to Jumper, but older.	Hands on hips, legs spread, shoulders back	
John Lennon				

DISCUSSION AND ANALYSIS

THE WORLD OF *CUT SNAKE*

A discussion of the world of a play should include reference to: location, time period, and context.

Cut Snake is set primarily in a non-specific Australian town, and relocates briefly to a range of locations all over the world.

> *We like to think the kids have grown up somewhere regional—like Castlemaine or something—but we also didn't want to specify a location exactly. We wanted it to feel like they could have been from anyone's home town.*
>
> DAN GIOVANNONI, co-writer

The audience are given a few references to time: Bob says he is born in 1986, and goes fishing with Tim (his grandson) in 2046. He also says that he was 19 when Jumper died. From this information, can you work out a rough time period for the play?

WHAT DO YOU THINK?

- What makes this a contemporary story?
- What elements of production (stagecraft elements) are there to help establish the world of the play?

STRUCTURE

> *Structure is important in any play, but especially in a play where you move back and forth through time. We needed to be sure it made sense, that the audience knew what time period we were in, and that it helped us tell the story.*
>
> DAN GIOVANNONI, co-writer

WHAT DO YOU THINK?

- In what way does the structure support the themes of the play?
- How is time used in the structure of the play? Is it disjointed? Linear?
- Where do you see the following conventions used in the performance:
  - Montage
  - Disjointed time sequence
  - Vignette
- Are they used appropriately? How do they help contribute to the telling of the story?

Catherine Davies as Kiki Coriander, Julia Billington as Bob and Kevin Kiernan-Molloy as Jumper in the 2013 Arthur production of *Cut Snake* at Rock Surfers Theatre Company, Sydney. (Photo: John Feely)

PERFORMANCE STYLES

NON-NATURALISM

We were influenced by many different performance styles. It's overwhelmingly non-naturalistic, and we've borrowed from a lot of practitioners and methodologies.

When writing, we wanted to have the best of both worlds— the satisfaction of a story well-told that you get from a play, combined with the excitement of physical theatre and the fun of the circus.

AMELIA EVANS, co-writer

WHAT DO YOU THINK?

- Describe and analyse how the elements of non-naturalism are used in *Cut Snake*. You could consider:
  - The use of direct address
  - The use of dance sequences and movement
  - The way sound is used to help create mood
  - The episodic structure
  - Disjointed, non-linear time sequences
- Identify any other performance styles you recognise in *Cut Snake*.
- Discuss how *Cut Snake* uses elements of the following performance styles or dramatists and how these contribute to the development of the performance:
  - Grotowsky
  - Suzuki
  - Commedia dell'Arte
  - Non-Naturalism
  - Brecht
  - Physical theatre
  - Magic Realism
  - Any other styles you can identify
- Evaluate the success of this fusion of styles and techniques in creating a piece of ensemble theatre.

CHARACTERS AND EXPRESSIVE SKILLS

Each character has a different posture and hence has a different way of moving and gesturing etc. It is from here that a character's voice comes out. Whatever the physical choice I made for the character informs the change in my voice, as I'm moving about as this new character a voice comes out that I feel suits the body.

KEVIN KIERNAN-MOLLOY, actor (Jumper)

I personally find characters through movement—how do they stand? What physically might they feel most confident/self-conscious about? I find a voice that comes quite naturally from how the character holds their body. From here you can get specific about speech patterns and then how that character might behave in front of another character—i.e. are they attracted to them? Do they dislike them? Do they feel powerful? And then you can experiment with the opposite, because that's how human beings often operate. Oh, and to keep things exciting, certain nuances creep in—this also helps to distinguish between characters (not only for the audience, but yourself as well!).

CAT DAVIES, actor (Kiki)

WHAT DO YOU THINK?

- Think back and remember each of the characters Kevin and Cat played—what were the postures, movements, gestures and character voices that distinguished each one from the next? For each character, identify:
  - Facial expressions: a grimace, pout, smile, frown.
  - Voice: tone, pitch, volume, timbre, accent.
  - Gesture: expressions, physiological, cultural.
  - Movement: body shape, gait, tempo, posture, body language.
- Identify and discuss the expressive skills used to transition between characters. Consider the moment of transformation for each of these characters. For example: how did Jumper transition into Lady Godiva? He adjusted his body into what position? How did his gait change? What did he do to his voice?

ELEMENTS OF PRODUCTION (STAGECRAFT ELEMENTS)

SET

> There is no formal set design for Cut Snake—because the show is so transportable, wherever it's being performed becomes the set, which is really just a backdrop. For example, we did it in a kitchen in a pub, so the backdrop for that performance was a weird 1970s kitchen. We also did it in a park under a tree, so the tree was the backdrop. We did this because the central tension in the play is 'ordinary vs. extraordinary'. We think the experience of the play is quite extraordinary, so we want it performed in ordinary settings.
>
> PAIGE RATTRAY, Director

Since the production has been touring, the creative team has developed a set that they can take with them.

WHAT DO YOU THINK?

- Sketch down what you can remember about the set.
- In what way did this production's set contribute to the non-naturalistic performance style?
- Discuss the concept of 'no design as a design'. Describe how you imagine the original production would have looked and felt.

COSTUME

> The costuming really came from a desire for the actors to be comfortable (they do run around a lot) and also to help create a really intimate vaudevillian or Commedia-esque sort of vibe—a highly theatrical aesthetic.
>
> PAIGE RATTRAY, director

WHAT DO YOU THINK?

- Evaluate the effectiveness of each character's costume. You should consider not only what the costume communicated to the audience, but how the costume assisted the actor with their transitions.

- If you were to redesign the costumes, what would you do differently? Justify your response.

SOUND AND MUSIC

In composing the music for the 'fairy' sequence, I used the rhythm from Steve Reich's 'Clapping Music' as an inspirational starting point, to compose something that could provide a pulse for the performers. You can hear every instrument playing on a loop, but with a range of instruments starting on different beats at different times; what you are left with becomes too complex for your brain to follow. This creates a dreamlike sound that builds and fades to follow the dancers' movements. Most of the instruments you hear play very percussive sounds, but they're all trying to play as quietly as possible. This creates a very intimate and intricate little work, painting a scene behind the dancers.

TOM HOGAN, composer

You can hear from the bus crash opening scene how intricately wound the sound is; with the script, movement and music all being developed at the same time, all the elements come together to tell their own part of the story. What you are left with is a combination of all your ideas, musical and otherwise, that had been developed right from the beginning.

TOM HOGAN, composer

WHAT DO YOU THINK?

- Evaluate the effect of sound on the fairy sequence. In your evaluation you should discuss the way sound can evoke mood and emotion.
- Describe the use of sound in *Cut Snake* and analyse its importance in relation to communicating the story to the audience.
- Evaluate the use of sound that accompanies Jumper's opening monologue (the bus crash). What mood or emotion does it evoke?
- Consider that the 'bus crash' theme is played twice, and a version of the 'tango' three times. Analyse the effect repeating music has. How did this help tell the story?

- Consider how Trix's introduction music contributes to transformation of place. Was this used to good effect?
- You can listen to the *Cut Snake* soundtrack and music online: www.arthurproductions.com.au/cut-snake-music

PROPS

We decided very early on that we didn't want to have lots of props. We wanted it to be highly theatrical, and that meant asking the audience to use their imaginations. Apart from costume pieces (masks, glasses), instruments (guitar) or characters themselves (the sock that becomes Trix and the Barbies that become the gypsies), the only prop is Jumper's journal. That had to be real.

AMELIA EVANS, co-writer

WHAT DO YOU THINK?

- Identify the importance of Jumper's journal.
- What does the writer mean when she says 'That had to be real'?
- Did you notice how many items were mimed instead of props being used? Evaluate the effectiveness of this lack of props in relation to the non-naturalistic style of the performance?

PUPPETS

The main ingredient, and what I relied on the most when bringing Trix to life, was to forget about myself, and solely focus on the character of Trix—how she moves, how she thinks, how she breathes. Even though I'm not hiding behind anything when I operate her, the audience still forgets me because my focus is entirely on her. And then you just get creative and detailed: What kind of voice does a snake have? What movement quality? What are her habits? What does she like? What does she dislike? And very simply, what just feels fun to do as a performer?

JULIA BILLINGTON, actor (Bob)

WHAT DO YOU THINK?

- Identify how the use of puppetry assisted in telling the story of *Cut Snake*.
- What expressive skills did Julia use to help create the character of Trix?

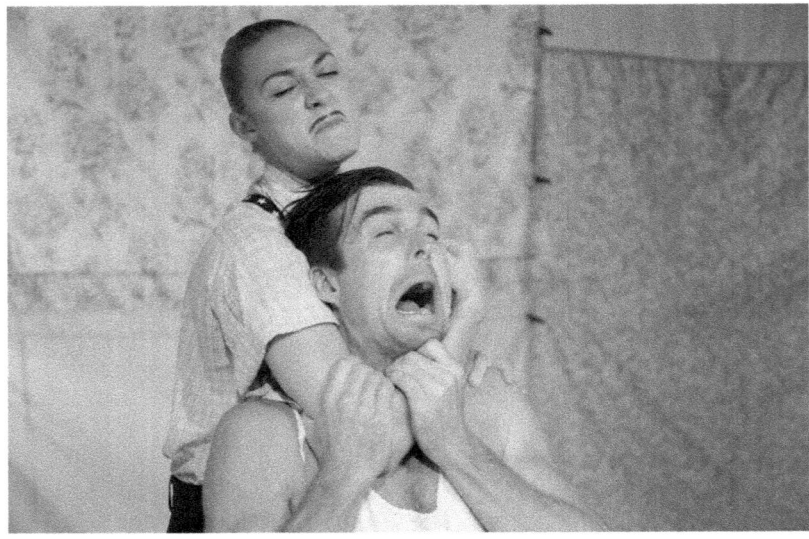

Julia Billington as Bob and Kevin Kiernan-Molloy as Jumper in the 2013 Arthur production of *Cut Snake* at Rock Surfers Theatre Company, Sydney. (Photo: John Feely)

ACTOR-AUDIENCE RELATIONSHIP

One of the first pieces of text we started playing around with was a monologue I had previously written. We read it as a group, and everyone really connected with it—the content as well as the form. The idea for having the story narrated kind of came from there—if Jumper could narrate his own death, then everyone else should get the chance to narrate their own lives.

DAN GIOVANNONI, co-writer

WHAT DO YOU THINK?

- In what way do the Narrator's opening lines help establish an actor-audience relationship?
- Describe the relationship the audience has with the actors onstage throughout the performance and identify how this relationship is maintained?
- Identify how 'breaking of the fourth wall' helps to tell the story of *Cut Snake*?
- How does the performance space affect the actor-audience relationship?

ELEMENTS OF DRAMA

Dramatic elements can be used together or separately to create a range of dramatic effects. Use the questions below to help you identify, evaluate and analyse how the elements of drama have been used in *Cut Snake*.

WHAT DO YOU THINK?

- In Jumper's opening monologue, what is the rhythm of the language? Is it slow? What about the physical rhythm? Is it the same? If so, what is the combined emotional effect? If not, how do the two rhythms juxtapose to create meaning? How does the rhythm of this scene create drama?
- Identify the central conflict of *Cut Snake*.
- Evaluate how the inner conflict develops and is maintained in the characters. For example, Bob's inner conflict might be that he wants to ignore the extraordinary things in his life but can't reconcile seeing the fairy. For Bob, perhaps it's a final attempt to resolve his inner conflict, which sees him invent time travel.
- Find examples of verbal, physical and non-verbal conflict in the play. As a guide, conflict generally occurs between two or more people who want the same or different things.
- How did you feel after the performance of *Cut Snake*? Identify the mood at the end of the performance? Discuss why you think the play ended with this mood?
- Identify three different moods present in the play. What dramatic and stagecraft elements were at play to help create those moods? Identify at least one of each.
- Identify and describe the climax of *Cut Snake*.
- What examples of contrast can you recall? Evaluate how contrast contributes to the audience's understanding of the play.
- Identify what symbols are present in the work? Evaluate the contribution of symbol in helping the audience understand the story?

THEMES

The themes of Cut Snake *became the big questions—the ones we couldn't answer easily, the ones that even talking about is hard.*
AMELIA EVANS, co-writer

WHAT DO YOU THINK?

- Below are some of the 'big questions' *Cut Snake* is dealing with. Describe how each of these questions is revealed in the play:
    - Can you ever get over the death of a loved one—especially a teenager?
    - How do you live an extraordinary life in an ordinary world?
    - How do you maintain connection with your friends?
    - How can you look to the future with hope when the adult world seems so depressing?
- Identify any other big questions that are present in the play.
- List the 'big questions' in your life? Do you think these questions are the same for everyone? In small groups discuss your big questions and identify any that are universal and what makes them universal.
- Describe and evaluate how the themes of loss and grief explored in *Cut Snake*.

EXTRA THINKING

RESEARCH AND INVESTIGATION

Consider how *Cut Snake* might tie into real-world events and scenarios.

Research the work of Australian palliative care nurse Bronnie Ware and her book *The Top Five Regrets of Dying* in which she details what she thinks are the top five regrets of her patients on their death bed.

- Discuss how the idea of regret is present in *Cut Snake*.

There have been a series of tragic accidents in the past few years involving young Australians on holiday. Research these accidents and choose one to investigate further.

- How might a story such as this contain links to Jumper's story?

SAMPLE SHORT ANSWER QUESTIONS

Performance Analysis Assessment:
1. Provide examples of how the themes of grief and loss are explored in *Cut Snake*. (4 marks)
2. Discuss three theatrical conventions used within the performance and give examples. (6 marks)
3. Select and list two characters. Evaluate how the actor used two expressive skills to communicate that character to the audience. (6 marks)
4. List three dramatic elements used. Describe how these elements assist in giving the performance its non-naturalistic style? Examine how they were created. (6 marks)
5. Name two elements of production (stagecraft elements) present in the performance and evaluate how effectively they were manipulated. (4 marks)
6. Describe aspects of the performance that can be linked to the influence of a dramatist or dramatists. Reflect on what this brought to the performance. (4 marks)

= 30 marks

SUGGESTED ACTIVITIES

PUPPETRY

Using only the things available to you in your classroom (pencil cases, socks, basketballs, etc) recreate the characters of Jumper, Kiki and Bob.
- Decide how you would represent them with objects/puppets?
- Describe how their characteristics are revealed through the puppets.
- Identify the performance skills would you use.
- Present your ideas to the class.

MONTAGE

What other periods in history might Bob have visited in his time-travel montage? Pick three events (real or fictional) and represent them:
- Firstly, in freeze-frame or tableau.
- Secondly, in a short vignette.
- Consider how you will transition between each time period.
- Present your vignettes to the class.

BEATBOX

In pairs, brainstorm your own list of questions that you would like answers to. These questions will form the basis of your own beatbox performance. In creating your performance, think about what Jumper and Bob did in *Cut Snake*—how they used their voice (pitch, in particular), as well as their bodies, to help them communicate the emotion and feeling of the scene.

www.ingramcontent.com/pod-product-compliance
Lightning Source LLC
Chambersburg PA
CBHW050025090426
42734CB00021B/3417